SLY FUNNY!
.. He will have parents in stitches!"

D1540583

About the Authors

VALERIE SHAFF's photographs have appeared in *The New Yorker*, *Harper's*, *Martha Stewart Living*, and *InStyle*. She lives in upstate New York.

ROY BLOUNT JR. is the author of eighteen books, including *Be Sweet* and *First Hubby*, and is often featured on the NPR program *Wait Wait . . . Don't Tell Me!* He lives in western Massachusetts.

Also by Valerie Shaff and Roy Blount Jr.

If only you knew how much I smell you:
True portraits of dogs

I am puppy, hear me yap

The ages of dog

Photographs by Valerie Shaff

Text by Roy Blount Jr.

Perennial Currents

An Imprint of HarperCollinsPublishers

To snips, snails, puppy-dog tails, and Noah
—R.B.

To Rex, the Wonder Dog
—V.S.

First Perennial Currents edition published 2004.

Printed in Italy by Milanostampa S.P.A.

Designed by John Kane

Library of Congress Cataloging-in-Publication Data is available.

ISBN 0-06-074712-9

04 05 06 07 08 ❖/MS 10 9 8 7 6 5 4 3 2 1

Acknowledgments

There are a number of people whose contributions to this book were invaluable. I wish to thank, first and foremost, my agent Janis Donnaud, whose clarity of vision, sensibility, and support have always made working together a true pleasure. I have Janis to thank for pairing me from the start with Roy, whose words resound in perfect harmony with my pictures. I feel privileged to be published in the company of one of the smartest, funniest writers alive. I was further blessed with being given Larry Ashmead as my executive editor—the fantasy come true of a worldly, witty, generous icon. Great thanks also to Allison McCabe, the editor who saw to the flow of all stages of production.

I attribute the quality of the reproduction of my photographs to the expertise of Katherine Pollak, who helped me print them, and to the discerning eyes and experience of Lucy Albanese, Liz Walker, Tracy Rao, Betty Lew, and Susan Kosko. Thank you, gals!

On a personal note, I am indebted to Kim Grega, who offered me a leap of faith when she gave me the opportunity to adopt my beloved "Ridgeless Rhodesian," Rex. Thanks also to Paul Schoengold, my tireless dog walker, whose understanding has helped me tremendously with my 100-pound toddler. Special thanks go to Elizabeth Salkoff and Carl Brown, Nancy and Nellie, Gloria Gilbert Stoga and Puppies Behind Bars, Guide Dog Foundation for the Blind in Smithtown and Guiding Eyes for the Blind of Yorktown Heights, Nicole Wesley Smith, Elizabeth Hess, and Sharon Gannon for essential inspiration.

Of course, this book would not have been possible without the participation of my spectacular subjects and their devoted people. Thank you all for your collaboration and enthusiasm.

Happy Dog Days!

—Valerie Shaff

Thanks to Janis Donnaud for bringing together the authors and dogs. We would all lick you in the face if we thought you would like it.

And thanks to all the dogs herein and to the people who are like members of their families.

—Roy Blount Jr.

Introduction

by Roy Blount Jr.

There is a school of animal psychology, I am told, which holds that dogs don't really like us, they just learn to respond to us in ways that induce us to look after them. Surely any psychologist who believes this is holding dogs to a higher standard of sincerity than that to which he holds himself. How can this psychologist have gotten to know dogs well enough to look into them without learning how to respond to them in certain ways that induce them to grant him access? Of course, maybe this psychologist doesn't really like dogs. In which case, no wonder he thinks dogs don't really like people.

I asked my friend Greg Jaynes what he thought about this proposition. "Well," he said, "I think Willie really likes me."

Willie, a female springer spaniel of what strikes me as heartfelt amiability, gave Greg a quizzical look. An ingratiating quizzical look, to be sure, but are we to deduce therefore that Willie puts on this look solely for ingratiation's sake? Is Willie just an actor? Well, so is Tom Hanks. Who ingratiates, I think most moviegoers would agree, *from within*. Otherwise, he would be Steve Guttenberg. Dogs *feel* quizzical about a lot of things, and one of them is why on earth people would worry about the question of whether dogs like them.

Okay, on occasion we may catch a dog falling back on technique. But consider my friends the Bettses' dog, Maxx. Being a male English bulldog, Maxx has only one facial expression. His body language is circumscribed by his being essentially a chunk. His vulnerability is limited by his not being afraid of anything. In his prime Maxx could have made a living, I am convinced, by taking prey away from wolves.

But whenever he sees me, he wheezes and huffs and flings himself into a frenzy of welcome. He has been doing this all his life, and he is eleven years old. In all that time, I have given him maybe eight or ten snacks. Petted him some, sure, but petting a bulldog is sort of like petting an animated rib roast. He could easily get along without me. Maybe he is happily sharing with me, an old acquaintance, his awareness that, on the whole, he has a better deal than coyotes. But I think he is just glad to see someone who is as glad to see him as I am. Such signals as I give him to that effect are not calculated, though I dare say they have evolved over many dog-positive generations, and I see no reason not to assume the same about him.

Now, consider this: In his prime, Maxx ate flashlight batteries, for instance. Tennis excites him so, he will run around and around and around the court until he collapses, loudly, just as someone is straining not to double-fault. He does his level best to hit people at the ankles so he can bowl them over and get them down to a level where he can lick their faces smellily. Once he ate a concrete block or something and then drank so much chlorinated water from the Bettses' swimming pool that Roland Betts had to drive two hundred and twenty miles round-trip in the middle of the night to get him to a vet who knows his history. If dogs are wily manipulators, why are they so often such a big pain in the butt?

The average golden Labrador is nothing if not ingratiating. And yet . . . Let us look at one case study, taken loosely from life, as it might be interpreted by the above-mentioned animal psychologist:

A canny young yellow Lab, Bob,
Considers it part of his job
      To chew up the shoes
      Of his patron, Ms. Hughes,
And vomit them up in a gob.

So well does he play her that you
Might think it has something to do
      With affection. In fact,
      It's all a big act.
Shoes, Bob would rather eschew.

However, a dog must get fed.
Inside that clever blond head
      Bob sees what he did
      As a nice juicy quid
Pro quo. And though nothing is said

To show how delighted Ms. Hughes is,
He's sure that his shoe trick amuses . . .
      Although, and it's curious,
      She *seems* to be furious—
But that's how a human enthuses.

So he lopes off downstairs to the den,
Where he's bitten three nice-looking men—
    Which certainly *should*
    Have done him some good—
Oh, what a sly dog he's been!

From catering so to his pigeon,
Does he feel unclean? Just a smidgen.
    So just for himself
    He anoints her bookshelf
With Bob's number one: his religion.

No. This is horrible. This is not the canine nature we know and love. Maybe this is how a cat acts . . . But I am not going to get into that. I like cats. Especially your cat. I just don't feel that cats, for whatever reason, are as forthright or as heedless of self-interest as a dog is or at least profoundly means to be.

    Which is not to deny that there are *issues* between dog and human that representatives of the two species need to sit down together and, insofar as humanly-caninely possible, work through. There are people and dogs, I suppose, who have trained each other so adroitly that they respond to each other's appeals with alacrity and precision. But the most poignant bond between person and dog is the tenuously but deeply shared sense that they so often, to their reciprocal wonderment, don't get each other. Valerie Shaff's photography captures not only dogs' innocent pleasures and clearly readable messages, but also many aspects of the essential canine bemusement vis-à-vis people.

Good dogs mean well. So do good people. But that leaves a lot to be figured out. A dog is very often the joint creature of skewed canine and human imagination. (See if you can guess which of the dogs in this book is Stephen King's.) So when a puppy yaps, we should listen. But we shouldn't expect to get to the bottom of what he is going on about by means of cold science.

Valerie Shaff, New Yorker, Nantucketer,
Visual dogcatcher par excellence
You seem to convey to us, Ms. Interlocutor,
What a puppy wants.

And also what older Rovers are seeking
Indoors and out, in country and city.
I've doggedly tried, in a manner of speaking,
To capture each dog in a ditty,

And have grown, if possible, fonder
Of dogs in the process of versification.
Thank you, each canine responder,
For your participation.

What?

Well yes I'm sleepy, I was up all night.

The few times I saw you it was: turn on the light,

"Please hush," and turn it off again. Great,

That was comforting. And I'm yelping, "Wait!

How can I make myself any clearer?

It's dark! I'm alone!" Can't you hear, or

What?

I'm a nice dog, everyone
Says so, and I *am*,
I'm a sweet little dog.

If I'd been bigger,
I'd've been bolder.
And now I'm older.

Wanna know who's a dog in her prime?

I'm.

My legs still feel a little rubbery.
Never follow a chipmunk into shrubbery.

You think my "crooked grin" is "darling"?
I thought I was snarling.

What you're looking at, here and now,

Is the dog that put the *wow* in bow-wow-wow.

One thing about people I find incredible:
Their sense of what is and isn't edible.
I just found something *extremely* tasty.
They took it away from me, said it was "nasty."

What's that? I've got
Dirt on my tongue?
And were you not
Ever young?

Hark! the number one dog hears
A noise before his friend does.
The alpha dog, with alpha ears,
Knows everything the wind does.

Who enters the world with the faintest inkling

There's anything wrong with spontaneous tinkling?

True, sand won't chew,
But it's fine to snuffle through,
And a challenge to your feet—you
Gotta dig it. So, at the beach you
Get sandy, don't you?

Yep, I'm a mama now,
Here's my pup.
Looks like his daddy's how
He'll grow up.

This one, I guess,

Will turn out to be

More or less

Like, you know, me.

When I'm stalking bumblebees,

Don't make me lose my focus, please.

One of our years is seven

Of yours, and do you believe

Dogs go to heaven?

Dogs don't. So we grieve

To see how undereager you are

To seize every minute.

Why would you drive away in the car

Without me in it?

You could say I have it pretty good
Here, yes you could.
But then too, you see,
You have me.

How did we get this way?

We're puppies, okay?

The whiskers, oh yes, people mention 'em,

Somewhat like a baby, his cheeks, people pinchin' 'em,

Bit of a bother, and they pull on 'em, too, they—

What's that, smell that?

There, that. Muskrat!

They don't interfere with the nose, now do they?

Hey!

Check out the saucy bichon frisé!

And me with my leash on!

Last night

It was "One more

Yelp out of you . . . "

And what, I'm through?

And now, you,

With the flash thing:

"Just one more."

Right.

I've heard that before.

Just don't ask me to smile for you, please.

I guess you think being a puppy's a breeze.

Nothing's so simple that people can't spoil it—
And they think *we* aren't quite bright?
If it is so awful to drink from the toilet,
Then why is it just the right height?

Charge! Where? Why? Don't know!

Just puppies got to go!

Ever notice how a ball

Sometimes will not move at all . . .

Playing possum.

Balls think you're so eager to toss 'em

They'll fake you out and then roll free.

Can't fool me.

Two little puppy dogs are we,
Speckledom and Speckledy.

Clover
Comes and clover
Goes, it's here and then
It's over till it's back again,
So: *roll around*
In it, squirm the sun-warmed grass down
Next to the cool ground
To make a bed both refreshing and restful.
A dog can lie
Still and sigh
And still be zestful.

Over and over I've rolled
In clover. It doesn't get old.

My personal wetness—don't you love it?

Here, because you're you, is your share of it.

Each small sigh serves to reiterate,
Nobody fits quite like a littermate.

I'm a big puppy, these are my slippers,
Neither one is this little nipper's.
I'll chew these up, and then chew him
Limb from limb from limb from limb.

I've got something on my mind and something in my mouth
And I don't know what either one is.

Not trailing anything definite right
Now—though we momentarily might.
Just hanging out, doing the hound
Thing, aromaing around.

What my brother and I

Want to know is why

As soon as people see us they seem to feel as though

They *have* to laugh and go:

"Teeny

Weeny."

I hear them say that owing
To my parentage, "No way of knowing
What kind of dog he'll be."

Me.

I leap at leaves . . .

Won't leave the trees . . .

Now fall, will you, fall!
I'll get you all!

What about this, now?

Puppies on a roof.

Here's what puppies think:

"Woof!" "Woof-woof!"

Right here beneath his chair's where I
Belong the most,
And if I die
Beneath his chair I won't be lost.

When I'm beside
The seaside I'm outside
Enough to get all of
My inside out.

I'm doing this for you, you know.

My heart is pounding. Does it show?

You've resolved to set aside an hour every evening to groom

Whom?

Aren't I as scrumptious as a dog can get

Yet?

There's much to be smelled in, say, your shirt,
But nothing's as good for a puppy as dirt.
Nothing fills my nose like earth
I stretch out on for all I'm worth.

There is so *much* dirt.

And I can touch dirt

In ways, *okay*, I can't your chair.

For a puppy dirt is always there.

I'm *not* "doleful,"
It's just my appearance.
I am soulful.

Then there's my earance.

If people want to treat me like a doll or
Something—check this collar.
Think I'm soft?
I've chewed three of these boys off.

I am puppy, hear me yap,
No, I won't get in your lap,
I've got other things to do,
For instance, bark at you
Because you want to get
My puppy doll, I bet.

Just try it.

So good to chew on
You want you one.

Just try it.

What's so funny? It had better

Not be how I look in this sweater.

Fuzzy?

Okay, I'm fuzzy.

And you're . . . ? Fond.

You got food?

Good.

Let's bond.

As a pup, of course, I scattered

Birds in all directions—flattered

By how they fluttered.

Knowing, now, how my bread is buttered,

I am pleased that I can

Serve as a guide to "game" for the man.

Whatever's approaching

Is not, I suppose,

A grizzly, but

One never knows.

Yes, I'm sweet,
I have to be.
If I weren't sweet
You'd think of me

As something other
In your house.
I saw you shudder
At that mouse.

I've got things down pretty well pat.

They love me here, I can live with the cat,

I know three ways to get under the fence,

And the shape I'm in is tip-top, hence

Life is sweet from here on out.

What do old dogs *sigh* about?

Now it's hot,
Now it snows.
What is "it"?
No one knows.

Again the charm
Of when it's warm
Is back and I'm
Still here this time.

For the moment, pleasant enough is
Sitting here on whatever this stuff is,
But odors waft upon the wind to
Portend wild things I will get into.

MORE FROM VALERIE SHAFF, ROY BLOUNT, JR., AND THOSE WONDERFUL ANIMALS!

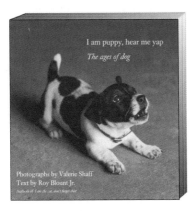

I Am Puppy, Hear Me Yap
The Ages of Dog
ISBN 0-06-074712-9 (paperback)

From sleepy golden retriever pups to sophisticated poodles, personality shines through in each of Shaff's remarkable photographs. Paired with Blount's puppy poetry, this book is, until dogs learn to talk, the best way to understand the "inner puppy" in all of them.

I Am the Cat, Don't Forget That
Feline Expressions
ISBN 0-06-056041-X (hardcover)

A witty and insightful look at America's other favorite pet—the cat. Shaff captures the essence of the ever-elusive cat and Blount's accompanying verse seems to speak their thoughts. The result is a touching and often hilarious take on the minds and hearts of felines.

Am I Pig Enough for You Yet?
Voices of the Barnyard
ISBN 0-06-019487-1 (hardcover)

Sure, we've all gazed at sheep and cows in fields by the sides of the road. But did you ever stop to think that perhaps they're looking back at YOU? And thinking some pretty funny things, too. Here, a charming collection of adorable farm animals—geese, llamas, pigs, sheep, mice and many more—romp through these pages, accompanied by hilarious verse.